UNCERTAINTIES AND REST

# UNCERTAINTIES AND REST

Poems by Timothy Steele

LOUISIANA STATE UNIVERSITY PRESS

*Baton Rouge and London*    1979

Acknowledgment is made to the following publications in which some
of these poems first appeared: *Poetry* ("Wait," "Homecoming in Late
March," "Three Notes Toward Definitions"), *Southern Review, Modern
Occasions, Counter/Measures, PN Review* (Great Britain), *Southern Hu-
manities Review, Chowder Review, Southern Poetry Review, Sequoia*, and
*Greensboro Review*.

Design: Dwight Agner
Typeface: VIP Bembo
Composition: LSU Press
Printer and binder: Thomson-Shore, Inc.

LIBRARY OF CONGRESS CATALOGING IN PUBLICATION DATA

Steele, Timothy.
  Uncertainties and rest.

  I. Title.
PS3569.T33845U5      811'.5'4      78–15063
ISBN 0–8071–0480–9
ISBN 0–8071–0481–7 pbk.

Publication of this book has been supported by a grant from the
National Endowment for the Arts in Washington, D.C., a federal
agency.

*For Brad and Martha*

# CONTENTS

# I  *Suburbs of the Sea*

# WITH A COPY OF RONALD FIRBANK

So much for dreaming. Light winds still distress
The fragrant shrubs and elegant parterre,
But in the palace court, His Weariness
The Prince is just a presence on the air.

Nor are the cellars filled with Grand Marnier.
And gone, alas, the celebrated guests:
Carmen Etoile, Pirelli, the coryphée,
The daughter of the famous flagellists.

In the obscurity, such innocence.
"What every soldier knows is understood."
Tag-ends of belief, dialogue, stock scenes—
Yet the books were, however minor, good.

Good but neglected. Or was that a part
Of the design? Even the Queen could see
Fame tends to be "très gutter," and that art
Is often just pretentious fantasy.

And though the mannerisms seem somewhat thin,
The kingdoms, in decline, are always there.
And even if they weren't, the novelist
Would understand. Or simply wouldn't care.

# SUNDAY AFTERNOON
*adapting a line from Alexander Barclay*


"Winter is near and the world is too hard."
And the phone, one might add, is disconnected.
In the tame isolation of my yard
I rake the last leaves. To be respected

And loved made sense to me once, but of late
I'm drawn by more workable conceits;
And the stiff, rooftop antics of a kite
And the leisure of broad, deserted streets

Seem to outweigh the needs of sentiment.
The clouds shift, the light alters, and I pass
Serenely through the afternoon, intent
On nothing but the leaves and the dead grass.

So calm, so settled. Such peace is the best.
And sheltered in the remnants of the day,
I gather what I want, and leave the rest
To the vague sounds of traffic, far away.

# PROFILS PERDUS

*for T.R.*   *"For him, only the evanescent existed; no substance, no tradition;*
              *just a spirit of travel, the moment."*

It does not matter if in Rome that fall
You, leaning on the rail of the balcony,
Watched a young woman pace the yard below,
Her parasol
Now raised, now shouldered. Nor need you feel, see,

More in the sudden rain which, in Marseilles,
Forced you into that church than the stained glass,
Or the four white candles, or the vast stillness,
Or the way
The marble echoes rippled through the Mass.

Nostalgia is your last, your perfect, fate.
In the vague wash of circumstance, you know
That any instant can in you assume
All the weight
And feeling of the absolute. And so,

What matters, simply, is that you contain
Both past and future; that sometime, somewhere,
You will yourself become the moment—an
Indefinite rain,
A profile disappearing in the air.

# STARGAZING AT BARTON

For the child who leans out over
the sill, mindful of the curtains,
may these stars be names remembered:
Taurus, Orion, and The Bear—
tranquil distances and moon-hung
bazaars the gods once frequented.

When Pascal speaks of "nothingness
from which we're drawn, infinity
in which we're swallowed up," he does
not mean this mid-August sky, this
quiet of meadows that has the
power to calm us. The alder

in the yard rattles in the wind;
and, from the woods, the rumble and
rush of a brook. Surely, we live
and care how we live. Undimin-
ished by our old contemplation,
the starlight remains fugitive

and beautiful, if only for
the child who loves it as it is,
who sees, leaning across the sill,
Taurus, Orion, and The Bear,
masters of their ancient distance,
bright and fading, immutable.

# SUBURBS OF THE SEA

## I *Evening, After the Auction*

Now nothing on the lawn but a cane chair
Of dubious value, and a paper cup
Capsized by the rose bush. The auctioneer
Stands on the sagging front steps, adding up

The profits for the late Miss Randel's heir.
The dead survive in trust and metaphors,
And she'd no doubt be proud to see what care
Went into this, how much that chest of drawers

Cost in the public dusk. The past, for hire,
Is still the past—though with a paradox:
In time, the worthless and the old acquire
Commercial dignity. The elm-lined walks

Flatter the secondhand and the beautiful,
As the auctioneer knows. If there is no mark
Of better times, at least the air is cool
And the lawn empty as the sky grows dark.

## II *History of a Friendship in Mattapoisett*

It starts with sherry and an armchair cruise.
    Then, nights in front of the fire screen;
Sap bubbling from the logs, there's coffee and
    The comforts of occasional news—
The wedding of a friend, books read, films seen.

Formality's a renewable disguise,
    Well-worded distance. Fog rolls in;
The tide turns. In this suburb of the sea,
    We do not over-analyze;
    We take on faith what we have been.

This morning, in your absence, scratch pads fill
    With curlicue and arabesque.
Slowly, appropriately, the fire sinks;
    Dust gathers on the window sill;
    And I clear papers from my desk,

My thoughts my own as rain drips from the eaves.
    Tact is at once acquired and shed:
In ending or beginning, it is natural
    To ask for certain clarities.
But something, always, must be left unsaid.

III  *A Couple, A Domestic Interior*
    on a photograph with the inscription: Vermont, 1903

Everything's focused: the globe lamps declare
a rolltop desk and bookcase; the grained air
is still. She is sewing; he looks on,
mustached and casual—though he clearly knows
that at any moment the shutter will close.

She appears somewhat cautious, too, but why?
Nothing's out of place. Curled on the floor,
their setter; and on the far wall, his portrait
and two oval mirrors that amplify
the harmony and light. Or is there more?

8

A mistress in Sherbrooke? some land deal he
pulled off to pay a gambling debt?
And on her side—a son who hates her? the
persistent fear of growing old alone?
a lover from her youth she can't forget?

Or is it merely that there's something tense
and forced about their innocence,
a willed denial of living? Still,
they look so solid, as if they knew
they'd only have to hold their pose until

the camera flashed once—and then they'd be
not simply granted security,
but fixed forever in the quiet here:
a man, a woman, a long afternoon,
calm, domestic, perfectly clear.

IV *Summer Fairytale*

It's once upon a thirty-first of June,
    A small man spinning straw to gold;
And we beguile the minor afternoon
Amid a wilderness of hollyhocks,
    While, elsewhere, princes climb to old
Disasters via fair Rapunzel's locks.

We find our peace in evenings of croquet,
    The thought of Gretel in her clearing;
Yet when the late sun glitters on the bay,
And overhead the seagulls wheel and pass,
    We grow abstracted, barely hearing
The click of ball and mallet on the grass.

9

Lord knows we need the past, but by degrees
      It can become a dubious spell;
Enchanters who once conjured mysteries
Now offer only ways of looking back,
      As though across the ocean's swell,
Or down alleys through the pine and tamarack.

The story, stripped of legend, will abide.
The Queen, however, wearies of distress;
The Prince ignores the spells the witches plied;
And we, although still drawn to the disguise
      Of our remembering, nonetheless
      Must wish our aging otherwise.

# THE MESSENGER

Of you, messenger, we ask only
Some intelligence of the weather
Or crops, or word from relatives in
The next village. These mornings, thin smoke

Rises from the chimney of the house
Across the valley. Late asters bloom
By forest pools black with reflected firs,
And never have our lives been so rich.

Do not then bring us tidings of wars
To the north, frozen rivers, passes
Blocked with snow. Enough that, certain nights,
We hear the osier clicking in wind

And sense all catastrophes you bear;
Enough that once we gave a stranger
Confidences of a nature that
Wiser men would never commit to

Another's keeping. We recognize
Shadow where it falls. Yet, messenger,
Know when you come that we will greet you
With all suitable formality;

Know that for you our table is laid,
The dark wine broached. Grow warm at our fire
And, when you are ready to, speak. We,
Bearers of other lives, will listen.

# INCIDENT ON A PICNIC

At length we tired of arguing, and drank
What little wine was left.
I leaned back on a bank
Of clover, and still thinking deft

Ripostes to what you'd said,
I noticed by the field below
A girl of ten or so
Who leaned across the pasture bar and fed

A calf a handful of grass.
You saw her too—and (I could see)
Felt the same shame that ran through me.
Did our self-serving angers pass

From us that moment? I can't say,
But I know that walking home that day
We weren't too certain or too proud
To note the roadside scent of hay

And the sky's white ribs of cloud.

# LEARNING TO SKATE
*for Pam Newton*


Back on the beach, your uncle's Irish setter
  Gallops, ears flapping, through the snow;
  I clutch a handful of your sweater
And half-contriving balance, let you tow

Me to the wide mouth of the bay. We sight,
  In turn, gray fishing huts, buoys caught
  In the clear ice, a streak of white
In the sky above the mountains of New York.

Arms swinging easily, you pick up speed;
  I let go, and now coast upon
  The blue-black darkness, as if freed
Of everything but air. Later on,

Returned to shore, I lean against a boulder;
  Hunched over, you unlace your skates.
  And there (above, beyond, your shoulder)
A young girl's doing figure-8's

One after another, her long red scarf streaming,
  Three, five, seven—ten or more!
  *I'll do that, too*, I think, daydreaming
In January, 1954.

# FOR MY MOTHER
*Barton, Vt.*


It was late August. Standing by the well,
I watched you gather wildflowers in the brake.
Red clover, goldenrod, and camomile,
The dragonflies and sunlight in the air—
And you waist-deep in all that color there.
So young, you seemed then. There was hay to make

And a cloud shadow on the Stevens' hill.
We two had grown apart, but I could see,
That moment, what you once were, and are still.
Only the light could touch you. The divorce,
Your father's death, the hard years: these, of course,
Were there, too. But your curiosity

And quiet were as wild as weeds, set off
From all the past. Mother, I know your ways:
Colombian prints; the mild defensive cough
You fill a silence with; that picnic ease,
Talk, and a paper plate poised on your knees.
Yet I was startled. Innocent of days,

How much of pain and learning we survive!
And I, discovering what I'd known before,
Stood silent in your calm, the light alive
And perfect as you finished your bouquet,
The wind and the long grass rippling away.
Nor did I call you. Nor could I ask more.

# II  *An Interlude of Epigrams*

1

Here lies Sir Tact, a diplomatic fellow
Whose silence was not golden, but just yellow.

2

It's Lance's goal in life and bed
To make his mistresses believe
Regardless of his nakedness
He's always something up his sleeve.

3

You asked me in to dine, and now just talk
Of Hegel, Mozart, a Picasso nude.
Your learning's splendid, but it's ten o'clock—
You've lots of food for thought, now where's the food?

4 *Pal*

When we're together you invariably ask
Advice and consolation. I don the mask
Of sympathy, lips pursed as you run through
Tales of misfiring conquests, a snafu
Involving an irate Ms. and a Mrs.
Who teaches yoga. What a sad world this is!
So difficult, so fraught with complication!
Concluding, you express appreciation:
*So kind of you to always hear me out,*
*I need a friend, a true friend.* Well, no doubt,
Yet if I ever speak to you in kind, you
Grow nervous, tense; my problems just remind you

Of meetings that you're late for. *So distressing*
*Your situation, yes, but I've this pressing*
*Engagement.* . . . Fair enough. But you should know
I've wearied of this curious quid pro quo.
You talk, I listen; when I talk, you flee—
And I'm afraid, though it much troubles me,
I'd best forego the joys of our relations
Henceforth. As for your future lamentations,
One listener should prove as good as another.
It's not a friend you need, friend, but a mother.

5 *Elegy for a First Novel*

Small book, that struggled to withstand
The flourish of my eager hand,
Forgive the plotless, fatal welter
Of the youth I tried to shelter.

6 *Reading Habits*

"He saw books through me." *Jane Eyre*

A devotee of Sylvia Plath,
She had a mildly chilling laugh.
I offered her Donne, Ralegh, Martial,
But she declined them, being partial
To "modern life"—surrealist dreams,
The existential at extremes,
Group sex and its well-planned disasters.
I wound up with Johnson's Masters.

## 7  *A Million Laughs*

No one can out-lampoon, -joke, -quip, or -pun you,
But the funnier you get the more we shun you.
The moral, sir? He who possesses wit
Should also have the sense to ration it.

## 8

Rake swears he'll settle down, reform,
And claims that, given time to choose,
He'll take a wife. Rake take a wife?
Of course—the question being, Whose?

## 9

No human fault is lost on Fuss,
And he can dissect each of us
Neatly in terms of his own choosing,
Sly, irritated, or amusing.
You wonder who escapes critique?
Who in our circle's spared his pique?
Whom he approves of? None of us
Unless, that is, you're counting Fuss.

## 10  *Sunt Bona, Sunt Quaedam Mediocria . . .*

Martial, you're right. Even the best collection
Of poetry will prove, upon inspection,
A volume all too slender and too piddling
With some good poems, some bad, some fair to middling.

# III *Notes Toward Definitions*

# WAIT

Six beds in a square room: you give your name
And sleep for days. Then the comeback—the shame,
The Thorazine, and long walks in the sun
As thought retreats from the oblivion
It took on trust. And through it all, you sense
Only your ruin and fatigue as dense
As sleep. What happened? They won't answer you,
But just solicit your submission to
The judgment they'll "in due time" formulate.
And till then? Get some rest. Be patient. Wait.

## FOR YING LEW

There's scarcely time to sort out the debris.
I'm coming down too fast. Although I see
The same world, Ying, the records and guitars
Grow less appealing, and the superstars
Are starting to look somewhat old and hard.
The drapes balloon; the night spills through the yard,
Remote and random. Fortune? Trial and error?
A life of well-domesticated terror?
Yes, and a little more Marx and Flaubert
Won't alter anything. Friend, everywhere
What might have been intrudes. I could debate
Hypothesize, suggest, and speculate
Till the Messiah comes back, but what then?
I've broken once and I may break again.
Meanwhile, the other pilgrims have returned,
Friends and their friends. They patiently have learned
How best to nurse their public agony.
And they are right, I guess. I probably
Sooner or later will pay up my tithe,
Pack my unfinished poems and sell this life
For some dime store compassion and regret.
I'm child to neither gods nor devils. Yet
You always are right there, discreet and true,
And when I give up and go under, you,
For my sake only, will be asking why.
How will I tell you I have no reply?

# HOMECOMING IN LATE MARCH

Things change, of course: the girl next door, just turned
Twelve, now affects indifference and a bra.
And in the backyard, the snow fence is down—
Wind, I suppose. Yet out beyond the garden,
The leisurely shoots of skunk cabbages curl
Up through the loam. And there is still the creek
And the light rippling on the underside
Of the stone bridge. And so, an old peace? No.
But something, perhaps, on which the mind can close:
Impartial quiet, tentative repose.

# FAMILY REUNION

It is a country life. For supper, rice
And meatloaf. The blue china plates suggest
The past. Nostalgia, quiet and precise,
Is all we ask for and desire here:
At such reunions, mere discretion's best.
We eat, we talk, and afterwards we clear

The table off for an evening of bridge.
Over coffee, we bid hand after hand
As the sun sinks behind a birch-lined ridge.
Four clubs and double—and each card is led
Within the ease of conversation and
The resonance of what is never said.

Tonight good nature's served up family-style.
The children's problems, the insurance bills,
Are indexed in another place. And while
There is no real change, everything will yield,
At least for now, to vistas of blue hills,
Or the silence of a still and dripping field.

And it's a resolution of sorts. Staid,
Together for the past, if nothing more,
We share the same relaxing masquerade—
A life that's always gentle, never strict,
In which there's space enough for us and for
Lies we no longer care to contradict.

## CODA IN WIND

Now moonlight has defined
The agile spruce and fir,
And though we draw the blind
We hear their dark limbs stir

The mild, familiar air
That we would shut outside
If only we knew where,
Or when, or what, to hide.

# OVER THE RAINBOW

These days one sees a Kansas in retreat.
In former years, the talk was of corn, wheat,
That stillness of tall fields, but now it seems
Markets no longer matter. In the heat,
Grain elevators stand against the sky
Like prehistoric ruins. Oz offers dreams
And Garland's music, and yet one must ply

Reality as well. At the weigh stations,
The trucks rev up. All roads and cultures end
In time and space, and all destinations
In mere convenience. One need not care
That a young girl once saw these skies descend
In clear bright color and bright native air
To a true hard rain, miles away somewhere.

# COWBOY

There's nothing to the west but cold hills,
And the landmarks never change. Who's there?
No one. The walls shift. I take two pills
And keep sucking in the dust and air.

I'm the only native in this room.
For months I've been tracking elk and deer
Through coffee, regrets, and stale perfume;
Yet in this rarefield atmosphere

Of domestic vistas and quaint names,
I'm the shepherd of my discipline,
An unemployed gunman playing games
With blue weeds of smoke and mescaline.

True, I'll move on soon. But even then,
Half-assed and stoned, I'll in part be here.
The cowboy who always rides again
On the bare rim of the last frontier.

# THIS IS

This is a child's forest: moss
and stunted pine, the casual
arbutus. In the pre-dawn dark,
lichen glows on the tree trunks,

and then, among the trees, smoky
light, the ironwork of our breath
on the cold air. No rider passes,
no hooves recall the earth,

and yet I remember that in such a place
I crossed a frozen stream
and saw, through the clear ice,
dark trout, green weeds.

That silence was of the mind.
But now, far away, bees are swarming;
drunk with noon, they cluster
in the mouths of enormous blossoms;

and here, before us, the fern's shadow
quivers; pollen fills the air. Be
calm. Going, we make no sound.
Our feet do not feel the earth.

# THREE NOTES
# TOWARD DEFINITIONS

## I *Of Culture*

Culture. It's an ingredient used in making
Pineapple yogurt, Gothic cathedrals.
It's Isaac Newton's experiments with prisms—
Its opposite being, one supposes,
Fried chicken TV dinners, plastic roses,
Confessional novels brimming over
With soul and solecisms.

One also should record how closely it
And water are related. Tiber⟷Rome,
Greece⟷the Aegean, Dr. Johnson⟷tea.
And in addition, one might note
That it involves things beautiful (*e.g.*,
Fine thread, clear glass, a Mozart serenade,
A brooch of amethyst or jade).

Druids observing this or that eclipse
Surely possess it. So does Socrates,
Who calmly lifts the hemlock to his lips.
And those firm, savagely aware
New England matrons have it in their way,
As do Ben Franklin, Billie Holliday,
Shakespeare and Fred Astaire.

That none of this recalls M. Arnold's phrase
About pursuing light and sweetness
Should not concern us. The soul seeks completeness,
And throughout the bewilderments it's dealt,
The spirit seeks its proper scope.
Culture? It's life humanely felt.
(See too Politeness, Mercy, Hope.)

## II  *Of Faith*

A puzzling topic, this. Should be filed under
Assurance, Things Unseen, Intimations. Yet
For all of its obscurities, it is
Expressed innumerably in objects—*viz.*,
A pencil, a French cigarette,
Suspension bridges, drawings of the sea,
Etchings of Japanese severity.

Which is to say that all of the above
(Pardon, dear reader, the didactic vein)
Imply convictions that our lives sustain.
Despite newspapers, bills, the efforts of
The politician, *Something real exists*;
And we in turn, by faith, produce
A further something for delight or use.

Granted, too smooth a formulation,
But it suggests a certain truth:
It is the incomplete and unexplored
That often offer the most true reward.
(See Hebrews 11:1–33,
St. Augustine's *Confessions*, Pascal's *Pensées*,
Darwin's *Autobiography*.)

So, too, by faith one may be led
To recognitions of a wealth of splendors:
The fine blond down on a child's wrist,
A dark field sheltered by an arm of mist,
The puddle in the driveway which reflects

A network of bare branches overhead.
Which brings us to the point that faith respects

Even the values of a fallen world.
Rimbaud discovered love in the bizarre,
Duccio an opulence in the austere.
So may we, in inauspicious weather
Or inauspicious labor, be aware
Of an angelic gift—though angels are
Another matter altogether.

III  *Of Friendship*

Byron considered it *Love without wings*.
Others associate it with long views
Of hills and lakes. Still others tend to muse
Upon the darker side of things:
Stale beer, unanswered letters, or a pal
All too Shakespearean. (Cross references:
Iago, Enobarbus, Brutus, Hal.)

The standard modifiers aren't, alas,
Illuminating. "Steadfast" "warm" and "feeling"
Don't indicate the strength we need in dealing
With someone else's longings and regrets.
*True friendship never is serene.*
(Madame de Sevigne? Proust? Seymour Glass?)
Misunderstandings, vagaries of spleen,

All the minutiae of despair—
It is in spite of these one comes to share
Experience, and sharing it, confirms

33

The Other in The Other's terms
And not one's own. (Consult as well Restriction,
Patience, and Love.) Though life may be construed
As merely a Cartesian fiction,

We yet respond to its detail:
A morning by the ocean, the horizon
Asserted by a single sail;
The neighbor's Siamese; a fireside talk
(Preferably with evening come)
Embellished by refreshments which recall
The wines in Plato's *Symposium*.

Or putting matters in another way,
We might (again invoking Johnson) say
That friendship offers troubles we're inclined
To cherish. Solitude is bliss?
There's that opinion, to be sure.
But there are ills of heart and mind
Which only companionship can cure.

# AUTOBIOGRAPHY

It has, after all, certain advantages.
When one writes about oneself, one is always
Careful to do justice to the subject. Then,
Too, there's room for digression: "He was, perhaps,
More obscure than sublime" or "It was a privilege
To witness such confusion" or "A saint should
Never be too obvious." Vanity is
Condoned. The master resembles his dog, the
Writer his book.
               Consider. The most thorough
Biographer is merely an instrument
Of distortion. His history verifies
Only itself: the life must fit the plan. And
Though the real figure may be no more honest,
There is this difference: he and the reader are
Equally deceived, and his words define the
Deception. Or, as a philosopher once
Remarked, "True glass, however cracked or flawed,
Will admit light." The moral being, of course,
That integrity is inescapable.

# TWO FOR THE ROAD

I *Night Transit*
  Florida, 1971

A latter day June in the Everglades:
The bar is sheened with beer, and the local belles
Sip Pepsi to the jukebox serenades
Of Merle Haggard, the Stones, and Kitty Wells.

Folk-rock or country? I drink only gin.
At ten of eight, two whores in fine array
Arrive, and the farmhands start closing in.
Discreet, I turn and look the other way.

There's always room for more mid-century shit,
Or so I have been told. Yet when, from the bar,
An orange-haired waitress calls: Will that be it?
I gratefully nod, and retreat to my car.

My heritage or theirs? I scarcely care.
The road opens, and the night is thick and sweet,
And up ahead, there's only a black sky where
The full moon rises slowly through the heat.

II *This Time Around*
  8:37 P.M.

There's a turbulence somewhere west of St. Paul.
Strung out on distance and cocaine, I call

The stewardess. A warm towel, airline food,
And headphones for two dollars. Altitude

Offers an almost unrelenting ease:
The affair ends in hatred, the friend OD's

But does it matter up here? Moving on,
There will be other roles—Pierrot, Don Juan,

The addict maintained at a cut-rate price.
The plane jolts; the cabin lights flash twice,

And dim. But no real trouble. Motion, sound,
And space will sustain me this time around.

And later? The descent to a different night,
A way back here, another dream of flight.

# IV  *Sufficiencies*

# EVEN THEN
*for you*


These are formal days: crocuses,
A seasonal chill, wind in the urban palms.

It is dangerous to admit loneliness,
But this afternoon, the charities of sun and sky

Are not enough; my hands, my face, the most
Casual features of my life seem strange to me.

Was this ever a winter world?—snow falling
Through the cones of streetlamps, and someone returning

To an earlier darkness? I know only that
I feel I've always been here; that, even then,

Years ago, I was standing where I stand now,
Emptied of longing, waiting for you.

## DON JUAN:
## A WINTER CONVALESCENCE

Agreed: the orange juice lacked finesse
And character. He drank it, though;
It offered reassurance, more or less,
A sense of well-being as he settled back
Under three layers of calico
With last year's *Farmer's Almanack*.

Each evening he would stare across
The garden: arbor, row of spruce,
A fountain filled with ice, two urns whose moss
Was dusted with fresh snow, a weathervane,
And, there, the statue. Not Cockaigne,
But it consoled him—like the juice,

The warm quilts, or some turn of phrase
In an old journal. Lint on his lapel,
The doctor diagnosed his malady
As "something that would pass in a few days."
Which meant? He had flu, or ennui.
No matter: it was just as well,

For finally there was nothing left to share
Except the dull dreams of the unconfessed.
Dusk coming on, he'd simply stare
Out at the garden—that perfect row
Of spruce, that statue, and that snow—
Claiming there much more than he guessed.

# NIGHTPIECE FOR THE
# SUMMER SOLSTICE

The guests gone, I stack up the paper plates.
The folding chairs no longer look unstable,
A swarm of midges clusters and dilates
Over the picnic table,

And I recall *In country meadows, mists*
*Are starting their white conquest of the land—*
Lines written when I thought French Symbolists
Were part of a brass band.

The soul may suffer a fastidious twitch,
And yet such schoolboy verse seems fitting now,
This mothy, lilac evening being more rich
Than good taste might allow.

Sounds of a neighbor's lawnmower, the elms
Unstirring in full leaf, the squirrel that lopes
Over the dark grass seem of other realms,
Dream-worlds in which all hopes

Are granted a sufficiency of light.
What stars define the sky now day is finished
Define it of a world which, though in night,
Is green and undiminished.

# STRICTLY ROMANTIC:
# COASTAL TOWN IN MAINE

Myth of the tidal thoroughfare,
This mimicry of waves,
Antic driftwood, and now the air
Coming to rest. "The graves

Of the forefathers were such seas."
Just so. And in the haze
Of August, light shifts with the breeze,
And these seem merely days,

Miraculous and utterly
Unnecessary. Here,
The bells of Angelus will be
A voice; the sails that clear

The harbor will complete the sky.
This is the summer's course,
The natural becoming by
Returning to its source.

And it is always on the edge
Of endless afternoons,
Wind in the eelgrass and salt sedge,
Wildflowers in the dunes.

# AT THE SUMMIT

It was the wind, perhaps,
Snapping at my sleeve
That made it seem unreal.
By then the air had grown
So thin it hurt to breathe;
The sound of trees would rise,
And gather, and collapse
About us where we stood.
Below us lay the gorge—
White water and dark wood.

It was so close to ease,
That day: we had enough
Of openness and space.
In time the forest's sough
Died down, and we, descending,
Found poppies, a deer's track—
And all of it unreal,
Even looking back.

## BAKER BEACH AT SUNSET
*July 4, 1976*


This is a place the ocean comes to die,
A small beach backed by trash cans and concrete.
Bits of torn paper scrape the sand; the sky
Supports a few gulls. Words seem obsolete

In settings such as these. The salt gusts blow
The scent of marijuana up our way.
No bathers in these tides, and, yes, I know
I've written nothing in three months. Friends say

That there's still gold in modernist motifs—
But I've learned what too much self-scrutiny
Does to the spirit. Secondhand beliefs,
The palpitating soul: how carefully

We shelter and array these. Two jets fade
West of the low sun, and the Golden Gate
Shines with a kind of neo-gothic pride,
A bright colossus of the Welfare State.

Out there, the city tugs are busy with
The commerce of the South Seas and Marin;
But gulls shriek at a distance now, as if
They know the tide is never coming in.

# JOGGING IN THE PRESIDIO

A laughable and solitary art,
This running. Yet as I head toward the rise,
The snap of gravel underfoot is part
Of loveliness—of wind, Van Ruisdael skies,

That grove of eucalyptus just passed through,
And, here, the mobile shade of fir and pine.
Though wayside skeptics eye me, I pursue
Nothing particular, nothing that's mine,

But merely leaves brought down by a hard rain
Last evening, the clear wind the swallows ride,
And the grass over which my shadow bends
Evenly uphill as I hit my stride.

# CALIFORNIA STREET,
1975–76

The studio was too dark and small,
The building too Victorian,
High-ceilinged and impractical—
Or so I thought when I moved in.

Yet out back was a garden sweet
With laurel, pyracantha, rose,
And a stone Bacchus stood knee deep
In wild thyme, shouldering a green hose.

And when night came, the studio changed.
I'd light a fire whose glow would fall
Upon the dark-spined novels ranged
Shelf upon shelf against the wall.

The room grew larger then, more still.
I'd watch the logs burn down to ash,
Each holding its smooth shape until
Collapsing with a soft orange crash.

Outside the light rain turned to mist,
That dampness sheltering my retreat.
When a car passed, its tires hissed
Over the slick black lamplit street.

Sometimes those nights I'd take a walk
Around the neighborhood, and stop
By daytime haunts: the Deli on Clay,
The Corner Store, Sam's Flower Shop.

Or pausing by a globed streetlamp,
I'd breathe the wetness and the light,
My collar turned against the damp
Till I was wholly of the night.

# LAST NIGHT AS YOU SLEPT

The clock's dial a luminous two-ten,
Its faint glow on pillow and sheet,
I woke—and the good fatigue and heat
We'd shared were gone; and I, sensing again

Distance as chill as the light on the shades,
Was so uncertain, love, of our rest
That I woke you almost as I drew my chest
Against the warm wings of your shoulder blades.

# A DEVOTIONAL SONNET

Lord, pity such sinners. Monday afternoon
Is not the proper time for Augustine.
My saints are porcelain, chipped clair de lune,
Books and white wine. But don't intervene:
My chastity, unwitting though it is,
Is real; nor have I worshipped bitterness.
Jobless and on the loose, my share of bliss
Is simply that I've felt what I confess.

And what absolves me? This chilled Chardonnay,
A few letters from Cambridge and Vermont,
And You, who will restrain me if I stray
Too far from love I both reject and want.
And should this be "interpreted disease,"
Yours are such sinners, such apologies.

# MORNINGS IN A NEW APARTMENT

Neither the pauper nor the nouveau riche,
You waken to the novelties of dawn:
Velveeta cheese suffices here for quiche;
Your boots, one doubled over, rest upon
An orange crate shared by Zane Grey and Stendhal.
And should you mourn the cherubs on the ceiling
(Smirking and fat, whose latex robes are peeling),
Remember that location, after all,

Is just an opportunity you trace,
An offering of adventure and delight.
Note, then, the asters on the mantelpiece;
Dust off the candlesticks whose verdigris
Catches the sun. So casual a grace
Might save you as you are. It might. It might.

# RURAL COLLOQUY WITH A PAINTER

By noon, as I recall, the sky was clear,
The meadow drying in the wind and sun.
And the dark boughs of a hillside spruce in motion,
We sat on your porch drinking Hires Root Beer
As you expatiated on the notion—
Your cherished old Whiteheadean ideal—
That form and movement are, or can be, one.

From a black granite shelf, your spaniel watched
Crows angle toward the wood. Serene, you praised
Eakins and Hopper—your hands giving shape
To what you said: *The logical escape*
*From all the self's excesses is the real.*
And then with a mock flourishing, you raised
Your glass and, in a long gulp, downed your drink.

And I, although not quite convinced, could think
That those wildflowers whose names I'd never know,
The spruce, the hillside, and the field below
Would offer their concurrence if they could.
And then, if form and movement were not one,
It hardly mattered much there in the sun.
I think that Whitehead might have understood.

# ONE MORNING

One morning, rubbing clear the windowpane,
He grows coherent. The dark aimless rain

Becomes, abruptly, perfect thought; the jeans
Draped from the chair, that vase, the magazines

Scattered on his desk seem to draw within
Some final syllable. And who he's been,

Or what, no longer counts. The hours dispose
The silence and the light, advance and close

Into his will alone. Force? Harmony?
It is his time, whose coming even he

Could never quite imagine—simple, clear,
And endlessly complete. Right now. Right here.